Free-Fall

poems by

Dana Yost

Finishing Line Press
Georgetown, Kentucky

Free-Fall

ACKNOWLEDGMENTS

I wish to thank the following publications for first publishing these poems:

"My Super Power," "Obsession:" *Etched Onyx*
"The Lonely Stalk Their Front Room Windows at Night," "Wedding Photo,"
"Lavender," "What Holds You:" *Pyrokinection*
"Another Night:" *Perceptions*
"For Sara:" *Santa Clara Review*
"Hands:" *New Plains Review*
"Night Light for the Harvest," "Pontoon Dream:" *Split Rock Review*
"Bird on a Post:" *Superpresent*
"Rainbow," "Euthanized," "Teen-Age Days," "Hoops by Myself:" *Fictional
Cafe*
"Free-Fall:" *Scurfpea*
"In With Dragonflies," "11:43:" *Pasque Petals*
"Blue Flannel:" *Petigru Review*

Publisher: Leah Huete de Maines
Editor: Christen Kincaid
Cover Art: Dana Yost
Author Photo: Rae Yost
Cover Design: Elizabeth Maines McCleavy

Order online: www.finishinglinepress.com
also available on amazon.com

Author inquiries and mail orders:
Finishing Line Press
PO Box 1626
Georgetown, Kentucky 40324
USA

Contents

My Super Power

You're looking for beauty to take the place
of those who are not here,
so someone tells me, and I believe her,
because life goes forward even when
those we want around us are elsewhere.
Do you want a super power, she asks.
What would you do with your super power?
Beam my friends to my side, just for an hour,
so we could talk, laugh, hug.
That's a nice super power, a strong super power,
she says. And I feel good that she thinks that way.
Of course, it's hypothetical. Even more than that,
it's dream-wishing, fool's game, no matter the warmth
it gives me.
For people's lives go on without me. They make
their own homes, fall in love, raise children,
spend too many hours at work—all the things
I wish they'd give up to be close to me.

So what do I do to replace them, those I've
lost either to death or to the continuity of life,
to moving away from those who matter?
I must look for beauty, she says, in new places,
in new hearts. It's no search for the weak,
I say, and this is so. The world is cold, is turned inward,
and to crack it you need a will as strong as an ice pick,
forever chipping. You join new committees, stand in line
for concerts, eat ice cream at the town fair. Yet, you don't
always get honest answers, or things are brought up
around you, but not to you—those new ones you want
close to you only elude you, slide up, then around,
and it's not the same. Not the same as before,
not the same as beauty.

So you continue the search.
Beauty exists in the world, you're sure of this,
the kind you're looking for. The kind you once had,

the kind you felt in the longing hold of a friend
before you said goodbye for what may be the last time.
Beauty exists in the world. If not where you've been looking,
then someplace else. When you've fallen, your hands
have not buckled, but grown stronger.
Continue the search, she says. You won't find
beauty by sitting still, but by climbing the rock,
circling the tree, waiting in line for the art show to open,
photos on canvas, a wasteland turned into grace
by the way the lens settles on leaves in a pathway.

The Lonely Stalk Their Front-Room Windows at Night

The lonely stalk their front-room windows at night,
watching snowflakes fall
in streetlight shadows, silent,
a robe over their shoulders,
rolling prayers and pleas through the folds of their minds,
standing until weary legs say "please." Eventually
day, night, light, dark
become the same, days are lost, holidays missed,
the front-room window a smear of old dreams,
vanished conversation.
Feral cats slash by,
indifferent
to the fingertip tap on the glass,
pausing only to piss yellow
into the cold white snow.

Obsession

I turn myself inside out,
as if pulling my flesh outward,
but really my mind—
pulling it to the surface
to find out what's obstructing
it, what it is I keep thinking
about to the near-exclusion
of all else.
I examine my thoughts,
my recesses. I share them
with my therapist week
after week. Like a fog
settled over me,
or the return of low-grade depression,
or some kind of actual thought,
an obsession,
that's jammed in my mind
like a stick between the spokes
of a child's bike.

After a time, I decide I may know,
may have a clue,
but am afraid to pursue it,
for what it might say about me,
about my life and those in it.
Too dangerous, too damaging,
too damned tempting,
a thing dangling before
my mind like juice dripping
from a bottle, tempting
with its tastes and touches.
So I work on ways to turn myself
back inside, bring the thing
to a quieter, more remote place
where it won't steal at me
so much, won't say "come to me,"

with all the implications those words
hold. I work on burying them,
busying myself with other thoughts,
with life in the real world, tangible,
like polishing the wood on the dining room
table, like walking in the heat, breathing
in the warm air and sifting my breath
for aromas from the houses I pass:
lilacs or baking bread or the sweat
of a dog just finished with a walk.

I read about foreign people,
I read about history,
I twist at night in my bed, working
to think of tomorrow, not that thing
that tempts. I sleep and dream
of old work days, and wake to
new tasks, new words—cicerone,
for one—and drag my mind
through the hard work of another day,
where reality, while duller than temptation,
is better for me, safer, even cozier.

Another Night

Another night waking.
Another night the sweats.
Another night walking to the railroad bridge.
The choir of crickets and tree frogs,
an owl in the trees, something
my half-Lakota friend would call an omen.
Beneath, the river holds the gray reflection
of the moon, its face as tired as my own.

Another night worn.
Another night television's political clatter
from the street's open windows:
the seething angry, the gloating belligerent,
forever on the precipice of a shove.
But strength, as the song goes, is not the same as violence.

Another night saying I want to be strong.
Saying I want the strength in the mercy and forgiveness of the meek,
in the patience of the dispossessed,
in the hope of the beaten-down,
in how I used to be:
calm in a sandstorm, saying this passes
and I'll hold your hand until it does.

What I want is the strength
of the stone slipping without sound
into the river beneath,
in its ripples a constancy, a force
that reaches the banks, spreads downriver
through bends, cuts and bows
to places I have never been.
In its ripples, a constancy
that harnesses my frenetic heartbeat.
Within that stone's fall,
the strength to reach, within and without, beyond what can be seen.

For Sara

suddenly,
she's bleeding,
down her leg,
but she thinks,
this isn't me,
not me, bleeding,
but it is her, the blood has reached
her ankle, then her toes
and is running on the bathroom
tile, but she still thinks it is not
her, she wouldn't do this,
she's been in trouble
before, but never has
she done this, then her mother
is taking her to the ER,
where she gives her name,
only it doesn't feel like her name,
but someone else's,
someone she knew once
when she was a child,
when she was safe,
and the nurse looks
at her, says we'll
have you stitched
up fast, and she thinks,
it was that deep a cut?
And it was, made by her,
they say. They, including
her mother.
The stitching up will be
minor compared to what
comes next: two days, at least,
locked down in a BHU,

and all the assessments
and talking it through
and she still swears it wasn't

her, and now she hears talk
of a long-term commitment
to an intense treatment center
and she's so tired all she wants
is sleep and she sleeps on the concrete
floor that leads to the concrete wall
that holds up the sparse bunk
in her room and she sleeps on that bunk, too,
sleeps until her mother comes to visit,
to tell her we have options,
and she says this isn't me,
isn't me, and if she could only
be let go to find herself, the real
her, who is out there somewhere,
twirling her hair and running bare feet
through sand on a beach, that girl
who has gotten away from her,
if she could find her maybe
all this could go away.

Hands

Hands and fingers: rough, scabbed,
calloused, bent, thick,
hands and fingers that do the rugged work
of turning politicians' sweetly-spun
words into the things we tell ourselves we need:
bigger homes, wider roads, faster Internet,
the red-brick/tall-windowed monuments
to ego and legacy.
It is the work of the rough,
the work of sweat,
the work of danger, caught
in a trench in the cold-water gush
of a broken pipe, waist deep, rising.
It is the work of cuffing aside
the shit of others,
of the heave and haw
of the backhoe claw,
and the hands needed to
twist, shove levers and gears,
to crank loose a decades-rusted nut,
to yank free grain from a feedmill auger,
strong hands, thick fingers.
It all says tough.

Yet, it's the forearm that says tough
in ways I still cannot bear:
Back twenty years, in his Army sergeant days,
after the Yellowstone fires,
after the Nevada desert survival training:
simply in a machine shop
at Fort Riley, outside Junction City, Kansas.
Welding a motor mount back in place,
protected by face-shielded helmet, welder's heat-retardant coat,
but not seeing a gap between glove and sleeve:
three bullets of runaway slag—molten junk metal—
find that gap, bounce and sear down the inside of the sleeve,
melting flesh on the lower side of the forearm.

I want to say shit when I hear the story,
but he's past the pain by then,
home on leave,
slowly rolling up the sleeve
to show the scars: craters of dead flesh,
gray and pocked, like an old man's mouth.

I've shaken the hands,
been bear-hugged by the arms:
He could crush bone if it came to it,
I think.
But I've also seen him bent over a pool table,
limbo-leaning under the bar lamp,
the cue a cellist's bow in those hands,
master's tap bringing forth a note
that spins the cue ball and, like the touch of a new father,
taps the striped 12-ball into a side pocket,
cue ball knowingly stopping,
sweetly aligned for the next shot,
the one that means the trophy and cash
from the big tournament in Sioux Falls,
the title for which there is only one winner,
the one whose hands and fingers
leave shadows over the green felt
but never a scratch.

Night Light for the Harvest

Sickle-shaped moon,
polished,
as if its edges
had been whetted

                  and it had cut

what it had been asked to cut
then wiped clean

                  and hung in the sky

like a tool on a workshop wall.

Bird on a Post

Blackbird
on a
post.
Car turning
left, traveling
too fast
for this
residential
street.

What if
it hits
me, I think.
Will the
blackbird
sing
the song
of my life
or will
I die
unattended?

What a
thing
to think
on a sunny
Thursday
morning.
I whistle
a tune
whose name
I don't
remember.
I walk
home,
and step
into the
shower.

Rainbow

Through the window
the sun blew into
a glass of white wine
then refracted into a rainbow
upon the skin of lemon-pepper chicken
as we talked about Nazi death camps
and soldiers killed by sniper fire
in Vietnam. A teacher dead
in the recent derecho.
It was such a peaceful
setting for death, wasn't it?
The seven of us around the table
and one finally mentioned
amnesty for draft-dodgers,
and no one went berserk,
no one even disagreed.
We shook our heads
at the insanity of war,
at the cruelty of death,
and my classmate
posted photos on Facebook
of herself in hospice,
ready to die from cancer.
"I'll be here for the end,"
she said from her living room
couch, under a blanket. I looked
for a rainbow but saw only
red and yellow
and someone shot Custer
to save his life.

Euthanized

I don't need to be anthologized.
Just euthanized
For my own damn good.
Otherwise,
I'm likely to riot,
Burn something down,
Or burn my way into your heart
Leaving only a hole
The size of a prick from a dart.

Teen-Age Days

A carton full of shoes,
none my size. A full-ton
pickup, its tailgate removed.
Balloon men and raggedy
jeans. I run to the outskirts
of town, to where dust
meets the asphalt.
I squat in the bean fields
hacking milkweed with a hoe.
Swisher Sweets in my breast pocket,
smoked at a park in the country.
Someone stole my red
bicycle, rode it up the hill.
I kissed a girl in the basement
of my parents' house.
The smell of beer on my
mother's breath.
To get away from it all,
my brother and I threw a football
in the rain across two
lawns, neither of us saying
a word, just heaving the ball
in arcs that called down
the sky.

Hoops By Myself

On the basketball court
in the back yard,
I am shooting from the wing.
I am Phil Chenier
from the Washington Bullets of the '70s.
Then I am Norm Van Lier
of the Chicago Bulls, driving the lane.
These ballplayers from my childhood
come to mind when I shoot
hoops by myself. Maybe it is this
way for anyone.
A dog trots past, pulling its
owner by the leash: a St. Bernard,
clearly weighing more than the
50 pounds allowed by the HOA.
Should I report it?
I don't want to be the bad guy,
the snitch. I look the other way.
I shoot again but the prairie wind
carries the ball to the left, so far
it misses not only the rim
but the entire backboard
and bounds across the grass.
I fetch it and try layups
for a while to cut through the wind.
I am an isolato, to use an old word.
Me. Myself. I. Alone out here,
as I am alone inside, only
inside I have my books.
But my doctor says I need
the exercise, too. Man does not
live by words alone, she jokes.

On the basketball court,
I practice hook shots now,
like Kareem used to so
so gracefully. Mine bounce

and clank, sometimes go in,
sometimes fall off to the side.
These ghosts of the '70s
laugh at me, I think. "We'd
never miss as badly as you."
They're right. But they didn't
have to contend with the wind.
I lift a shot from the free-throw line.
It goes in with a swish. I pump
a fist. "Yes." Yes.

Free-Fall

to have no
>
> rules
>
> > no gravity

to free-fall above my mother's
Japanese garden,
above her patio table
>
> where she sits
with her coffee   and menthol cigarettes

to fall back in time   to see this
my mother who is long dead
but lives strong in my mind, my heart

to have no
>
> rules
to travel back   more than a century
find myself in the batter's box
>
> against the great Walter Johnson
fireballer sidearmer
and somehow tag one   take it deep
out of the ballpark and be cheered
>
> as a hero
even though it means breaking
>
> Johnson's heart
since he is still looking for his first World Series
victory which will not come
>
> until 1924   not in my
surprise at bat against him   I don't know
how to feel about this: heroic or dream-buster
bum to let down Johnson whose picture hangs
on the side of my book shelf   who died young
of brain cancer   to free-fall to such
a dilemma

to have no
        rules
             no laws
so when I pick a wild flower
up comes peace not just   in my heart
but for the world which is now up to me to
figure how to share   how to shake this plant
in every direction so that its seeds land
on everyone
peace for everyone
what a   dream
peace for you
this is what I pull from deep within the earth
when I tug at the wild flower
out in the woods
peace

no rules
        just that

how wonderful
even if a dream

Wedding Photo

One of my cousin's children dug it up online:
a photo and writeup
of my parents' wedding from 1959,
the photo showing my mother
at all of 18, smiling, blond,
glancing downward at the camera.
I wonder what was said
between her and the photographer,
between her and my father
on that memorable day,
between her and my grandmother,
who surely was worried about
the new hands my mother would be in.
I wonder if my mother had any
foreshadowing of what was
to come: the five children,
the eleven grandchildren,
the cancer that she fought
for eleven years then finally
stilled her heart. Even the second
marriage after my father died young.
If she'd had any foreknowledge,
would she have gone through
with it, would she have still
said yes and gone on to live
as she really did, with the good,
the hard days in front of her,
the days to be proud,
the days of difficult decisions,
the days of re-wallpapering
the big old house,
the days of sitting, worn out,
in the sun-room addition,
cigarette in one hand,
lighter in the other,
a deep breath,
then the inhalation
of menthol.

Lavender

In a marshy field,
park management
mowed down rows
of sumac, leaving
the hard roots exposed,
waiting to die.
It was a way to clear
off unwanted bush,
I suppose, and a reminder
that not everyone
likes everything that grows
—some see a nuisance,
some see something
unpretty that they are
content to let wither,
then fade away.
Life is like that, too,
and I feel a thud
in my heart as I stand
over the field,
a loss, an emptiness.
Later, we travel
to the Loess Hills
where someone
is growing lavender,
turning its oil
into soap, handkerchiefs,
wall art, cooking spice.
A reminder that the prairie
gives life, often in abundance,
and my heart rebounds.
I buy a kerchief, wrap
it around my neck
and inhale the fragrance.
It smells like prairie,
but more: like life itself,

and I want to lay
in the garden, butterflies
and dragonflies lighting
on my toes then blowing
where the wind takes them,
toward the hills, the sky,
toward freedom.

What Holds You

One of those days when you were sure
she was not going to live but a few hours more,
and you thought about your childhood with her,
you thought melancholy things,
you thought about her reading books
to you when you were two, three,
and the way that shaped the rest of your life,
you thought about walks in the small town
under elm trees that later died of disease,
and about how she cooked you white rice
sprinkled with cinnamon, not because it was
a delicacy but was what she could afford
on your father's meager pay.

You thought about losing her,
what memories you hadn't yet
shared with her, what stories
from her own path she hadn't yet
told you. But then she woke
from sleep and said she felt
better and she lived yet another
night and another day and things
continued on, and you still thought
the things you thought, undaunted by death,
because you knew it was coming,
would come and then it did,
and you lay there next to her,
as if waiting for another memory,
yet you felt nothing but grief
            beginning its slow, long
wend into your soul.

In With Dragonflies

How close to anger
can I come before I burst,
before I curse the infernal
stupidity, lack of care, lack of heart
of some in this nation
of ours? So selfish,
playing politics with the lives
of others, so misogynistic,
in the word of another writer,
that it leaves one longing
to spit in their faces, leaves
one longing for the power
to reroute the words of
those in power. But I am
a simple man, no office-holder,
no influencer. I take humbler
paths, the anger riding on
my shoulder like a quiet
passenger. I walk a park
trail near where I live,
inhaling the aroma of lavender,
looking for the woodpecker
on the cottonwood,
pausing to let a fawn
pass in front of me.
My anger subsides,
but not the urge to do something,
to invoke change, to make this
a better place. I lift a baby turtle
from the path, carry it to the tall
grass where it continues its
slow walk. I watch the blue
and green bodies of dragonflies
in the brush, sometimes popping
up around my face. In my anger,
I find room for wonder.

11:43

11:43 and something like sleep
is finally kicking in.
It's one of my pills,
pulling me under,
into light-sleep dreams:
a New York woman,
long and elegant,
black dress slit at the knees.
Dorothy Parker writing
about being an anti-fascist.
Me, out back, shooting
hoops on the playground
cement.
Then, darkness, but
I tumble, tear at
the bedding, I find
when I wake. It's
turmoil, twisted
and a-twirl,
wrapped around
my legs and torso.
What weighs
in my sleep
to do that?
It is not the
darkness of death,
then, but of a different
life, the unconscious,
I see that, yet nothing
tells me if I dance
with the woman
from New York.

Pontoon Dream

In my mother's house,
a photo of my father holding
a walleye in both hands.
My father grins, almost a proud boy again,
his eyes a squint under white cap.
I dreamed of this yesterday,
of my father knowing how to glide
a pontoon softly between reeds,
hover it over hungry fish,
use the right silvery lure,
and, with cigarette between lips,
give a light flick.

Blue Flannel

A fragment of a blue flannel shirt,
wind-frayed and snagged, hangs
in the branches of a red maple.
It's not mine—the shirt. But I pass
it each day on my walk.
So I claim it as a mental possession,
like a tick mark on a list of things
that tracks where I am in my day.

I need these things,
these talismans.
Otherwise my days
spin without catching,
like a broken roulette wheel:
no risk,
but also no purpose.

Dana Yost was an award-winning daily newspaper journalist for 29 years. Since 2008, he has had nine books published, with *Free-Fall* his ninth. He is a three-time Pushcart Prize nominee.

Yost primarily worked at daily papers in Marshall, Minnesota, and Willmar, Minnesota. Among his major journalism awards, Yost twice was named the state's best daily newspaper columnist by the Minnesota Newspaper Association, won the best editorial portfolio award in an annual MNA contest, won first place for writing about politics in a contest by the Minnesota Associated Press Association, first place for feature writing from the South Dakota Press Association and was awarded the prestigious Journalism Accountability Award from the Minnesota Newspaper Council.

Among his notable books are the history book *1940: Journal of a Midwestern Town, Story of an Era* (Ellis Press), and the poetry books *Grace* (Spoon River Poetry Press) and *In Your Head* (South Dakota State Poetry Society). *In Your Head* won the annual SDSPS chapbook contest in 2020. He also won the 2015 Reader's Choice Award from *District Lit* for his poem "Where the Music Died."

Yost received a bachelor's degree in creative writing/literature from Southwest Minnesota State University. He served on the Minnesota Associated Press Association board of directors and serves on the South Dakota State Poetry Society board and was previously its president.

He lives in Sioux Falls, South Dakota.

www.ingramcontent.com/pod-product-compliance
Lightning Source LLC
Chambersburg PA
CBHW022059080426
42734CB00009B/1411